P9-DMJ-872

LYNDON B. JOHNSON

# ENCYCLOPEDIA of PRESIDENTS

## *Lyndon B. Johnson*

*Thirty-Sixth President of the United States*

By Jim Hargrove

*Consultant: Charles Abele, Ph.D.*
*Social Studies Instructor*
*Chicago Public School System*

CHILDRENS PRESS ®

CHICAGO

**The president and the First Lady have the first dance
at Johnson's inaugural ball, January 20, 1965.**

Library of Congress Cataloging-in-Publication Data

Hargrove, Jim.
  Lyndon B. Johnson / by Jim Hargrove.
    p.    cm.—(Encyclopedia of presidents)
  Includes index.
  Summary: Surveys the life of the Texas politician who became
America's thirty-sixth president and faced great public controversy
during the war in Vietnam.
  ISBN 0-516-01396-3
  1.  Johnson, Lyndon B. (Lyndon Baines). 1908-1973—Juvenile
literature.  2.  Presidents—United States—Biography—Juvenile
literature.  [1.  Johnson, Lyndon B. (Lyndon Baines), 1908-1973.
2.  Presidents]  I. Title.  II. Series.
E847.H33   1987
973.923'092'4—dc19
[B]
[92]                            87-15890
                                  CIP
                                    AC

Childrens Press, Chicago
Copyright ©1987 by Regensteiner Publishing Enterprises, Inc.
All rights reserved. Published simultaneously in Canada.
Printed in the United States of America.
1 2 3 4 5 6 7 8 9 10 R 96 95 94 93 92 91 90 89 88 87

**Picture Acknowledgments**

AP/Wide World Photos—6, 10, 13 (top), 16, 18
(left), 28 (2 photos), 32, 33, 38, 41, 44, 50, 52,
58, 59, 65, 78, 79

Historical Pictures Service—54, 55, 60

Lyndon B. Johnson Library—17 (2 photos), 19,
21 (2 photos), 30, 34, 35, 39, 42, 51, 84

Photri—67

United Press International—4, 5, 13 (bottom),
14, 18 (right), 22, 25, 26, 27, 36, 43, 47, 48, 49,
53, 57, 61, 62, 68, 69, 71, 72, 73, 74, 75, 76, 77
(2 photos), 80, 81, 82 (2 photos), 83 (2 photos),
86, 87, 88, 89

U.S. Bureau of Printing and Engraving—2

Cover design and illustration by
Steven Gaston Dobson

30003000033082

Johnson speaks against the "dangerous" foreign policies of his presidential opponent, Barry Goldwater, during a campaign speech in Saint Louis in October 1964.

# Table of Contents

Lyndon B. Johnson takes the oath of office aboard the presidential plane
shortly after the death of President John F. Kennedy. Beside him are his wife,
Lady Bird, and Jacqueline Kennedy, wife of the assassinated president.

# Chapter 1

# Three Tragic Hours in Dallas

The airplane carrying Vice-President Lyndon B. Johnson and his wife, Lady Bird, landed in Dallas about 11:30 Friday morning, November 22, 1963. The vice-president and Mrs. Johnson walked down the steps from the airplane and were greeted by a group of dignitaries gathered at the airport. In the background, thousands of spectators cheered as the vice-president—born and raised in Texas about two hundred miles south of Dallas—made his appearance.

Minutes later, *Air Force One*, the airplane carrying the handsome young President John F. Kennedy and his beautiful wife, Jacqueline, taxied to a stop nearby. The vice-president stepped back into the group of dignitaries so that he, too, could welcome the president and the First Lady to Dallas.

Kennedy and Johnson had come to Texas to raise money for the 1964 presidential campaign. Although the presidential elections were still nearly a year away, both men hoped to be reelected to a second term in office. Already the long campaign season had begun.

After the brief greetings were completed, President and Mrs. Kennedy were escorted to a large limousine, where they joined the governor of Texas, John Connally, and his wife. Vice-President and Mrs. Johnson got into another limousine with a U.S. senator from Texas, Ralph Yarborough. Led by uniformed policemen on motorcycles, the presidential motorcade headed away from the airport and toward downtown Dallas.

The exact route to be taken had been the subject of some controversy. Members of the Secret Service, whose responsibility it is to defend the lives of the president, vice-president, and their families, wanted to take the most direct route available to the Dallas Trade Mart, where the president was scheduled to make a speech.

Vice-President Johnson wanted the motorcade to pass down the main street of Dallas, where the largest number of people could see the passing parade. President Kennedy followed his vice-president's advice and overruled the Secret Service.

Another controversy centered on whether the route should be kept secret. Secret Service agents did not want the general public to know which route the presidential motorcade would take.

But local Texas politicians, anxious to be seen with the popular president and vice-president, wanted to publish a map in the newspaper so that more spectators would be on hand to cheer the officials as they passed by. Once again, the Secret Service agents were overruled. The motorcade route was published in the morning edition of the *Dallas News*.

As the motorcade headed toward downtown Dallas, the presidential limousine was in the lead, followed by a car filled with Secret Service agents, and then by the limousine carrying the vice-president. Other cars, carrying local politicians, and a bus for news reporters, brought up the rear of the motorcade; police motorcycles and cars were everywhere. All along the route, thousands of spectators cheered, waved, and applauded as the limousines passed by.

The motorcade made a right turn as the road began to slope downward beneath a series of three overpasses. Seconds later, a sound like a gunshot rang out. From his vantage point in the vice-president's car, Secret Service agent Rufus Youngblood could not see exactly what had happened. But up ahead President Kennedy's car swerved sharply, and the president himself seemed to be falling to his left.

"Get down!" agent Youngblood shouted at Johnson. "Get down!" As the vice-president slumped down on the seat, the agent threw his body on top of him. The loud sounds of two more gunshots rang out. People on the street were screaming and running for cover.

The two-way radio in Johnson's car broadcast the urgent voices of Secret Service agents using code names.

"Halfback! Halfback to Lawson! The President's been hit! Get us to a hospital, fast but safe."

The radio crackled with different voices snapping out quick, hurried instructions. Agent Youngblood continued to shield the vice-president as the car lurched forward and began picking up speed.

The presidential motorcade passes the Texas School Book Depository.

Johnson, with his face pressed against the car seat, could see virtually nothing; but in minutes his limousine pulled up to Dallas's Parkland Hospital. Surrounded by more Secret Service agents, he and Mrs. Johnson were hurried into the hospital building, down a corridor, and into the first room in the hallway. Agents slammed the door shut, pulled down the window shades, and remained with Johnson and his wife while they waited for reports on the president's condition.

Johnson soon learned that President Kennedy had been shot in the head. Governor Connally had also been hit but was not in serious condition. Just before 1:00 P.M., a priest arrived at the hospital. Many feared that he was there to give last rites to the Catholic president. About twenty minutes later, the vice-president was informed that President Kennedy had died. According to the rules of the U.S. Constitution, Lyndon Johnson was now the president of the United States.

The first duty of the Secret Service now was to protect the new president, in case other gunmen were out to assassinate him as well. Under heavy guard, Lady Bird walked to the room where the slain president's widow Jacqueline waited in shock, and did her best to express her sorrow. Then, even before Kennedy's untimely death was announced to the world, the country's new president and First Lady were taken secretly to the airport in an unmarked car.

As soon as the Johnsons reached *Air Force One*, a series of radio calls were made to the White House. The new president needed the advice of the U.S. Attorney General, Robert Kennedy, brother of the slain president, as to how the oath of office should be given. Although grief-stricken by the news of his brother's assassination, Robert Kennedy offered quick, sound advice: the oath of office should be given immediately by a Dallas judge. No one on the airplane knew the exact words of the oath. A copy was found at the White House and read over the radio to a presidential assistant in *Air Force One* who copied it down on a slip of paper.

While everyone aboard the airplane waited for the judge, Jacqueline Kennedy arrived with the casket carrying the body of her husband. For everyone, the sight was almost unbearable. Her dress was still covered with her husband's blood, and her large eyes darted around in pain and shock and confusion. While Mrs. Kennedy tried to compose herself, Dallas Judge Sarah Hughes arrived to administer the oath of office to the new president. When someone suggested they proceed, Lyndon Johnson said, "No, let's see if Mrs. Kennedy can stand this."

Invited to come forward in the airplane to the compartment where the swearing-in ceremony was about to take place, the late president's widow accepted. Judge Hughes was handed the words, included in the U.S. Constitution, to the presidential oath of office. Lyndon Johnson, with Mrs. Kennedy to his left and Mrs. Johnson to his right, repeated the words spoken by the judge:

> I do solemnly swear that I will faithfully execute the office of president of the United States, and will to the best of my ability, preserve, protect and defend the Constitution of the United States.

Immediately after the oath had been administered, the engines of *Air Force One* began to roar. At 2:47 P.M., nearly three hours after it had touched down in Dallas, the airplane left the ground. Lyndon B. Johnson had become the thirty-sixth president of the United States. Even in his youth, many people had predicted he would go far in politics. No one knew that he would reach the nation's highest office by such a tragic route.

Above: President Kennedy's limousine speeds toward Dallas's Parkland Hospital moments after he was shot. (White arrow points to his foot protruding over the side of the car. Black arrow points to Mrs. John Connally, bending down to avoid bullets.)

Right: Mrs. Kennedy holds the hands of her children, Caroline and John, Jr., on the steps of Saint Matthew's Cathedral in Washington, D.C., after their father's funeral. Beside her are Kennedy's brothers Ted and Robert.

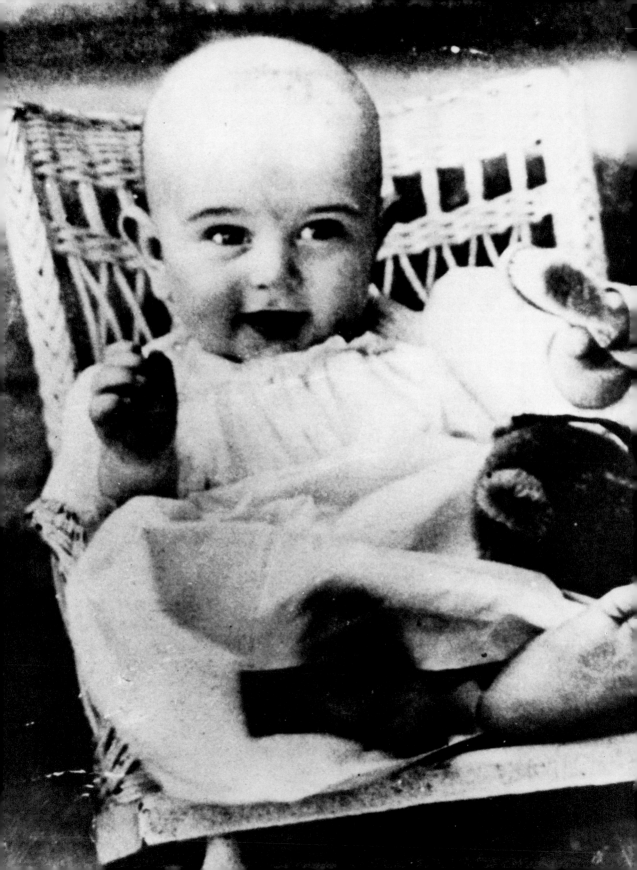

# Chapter 2

# Johnson and Johnson City

The night of August 27, 1908, was as stormy as many of the ranchers and farmers in the Pedernales Valley of central Texas could remember. Sam Ealy Johnson, Sr.—Lyndon's grandfather—rushed out of the family farmhouse into the stormy night to get help for his son's wife. Sam Ealy Johnson, Jr., and his wife Rebekah were expecting their first child. Sam Senior knew that it would be impossible to cross the flooding Pedernales River and bring back the nearest doctor, who lived twenty miles away. Instead, he brought home an experienced midwife skilled in assisting at childbirth.

Lyndon Johnson was born that same night, although it was some time before he was given a full name. For months Rebekah, one of the few college-educated women in the area, made long lists of names for the child and showed them to her husband, Sam Junior. Nothing seemed to please him. Finally, one morning in November, Rebekah refused to cook breakfast for her husband until he agreed to name their firstborn child. The name Lyndon was quickly settled upon.

**Opposite page: Six-month-old Lyndon with his teddy bear**

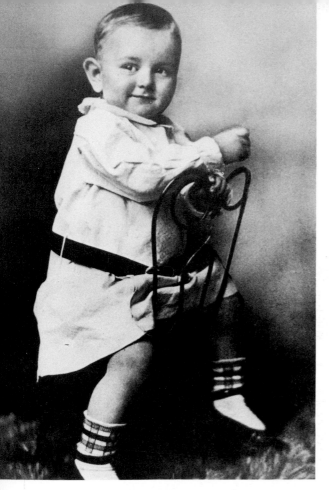

Lyndon at the age
of eighteen months

Every other year for the next eight years, Rebekah gave
birth to another child; but Lyndon remained her favorite.
He soon showed an unusual intelligence. By age three he
could read a few simple children's stories and spell a fair
number of words. He was also eager to learn more. Long
before he was old enough to attend the first grade, he wan-
dered off the family ranch to a tiny one-room schoolhouse,
where a single teacher taught about thirty-five students in
eight different grades. There, young Lyndon held onto the
skirt of the teacher and listened attentively to the lessons
she gave. When his mother learned about Lyndon's daily
visits to school, she got permission from the local school
board for him to attend classes.

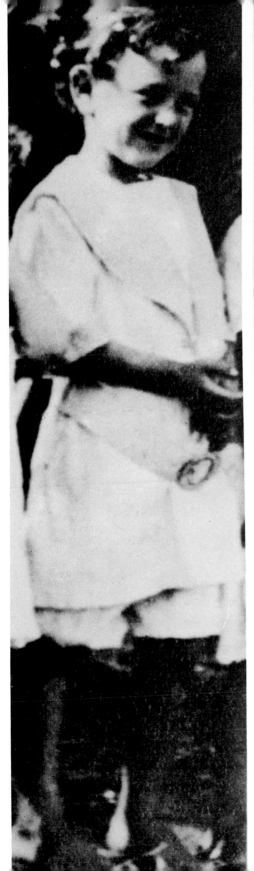

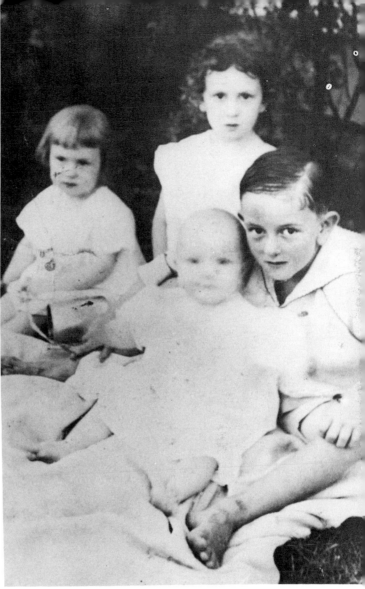

Above: Lyndon with his baby brother, Sam
Left: Lyndon, at four, had golden curls.

**Above: Rebekah Johnson, Lyndon's mother**

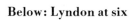

Below: Lyndon at six

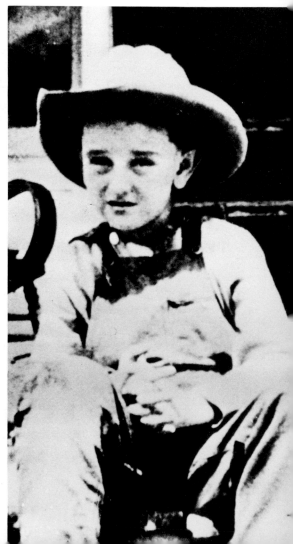

Sam Johnson,
Lyndon's father

Sam Ealy Johnson, Jr., Lyndon's father, worked as a cotton trader, a schoolteacher, a rancher, and a member of the Texas state legislature for five terms, among other things. In the scrubby hill country of Texas, it was hard in those days for anyone to earn a living. Sam had to struggle to keep his growing family clothed and fed, but the Johnsons were as well off as most of their neighbors.

When Lyndon Johnson was a grown man and a famous politician, he remembered his childhood slightly different-ly, especially when visitors were present. Whenever he could get away from Washington, he returned to his beloved ranch on the Pedernales River which he bought back from other owners when he was grown. There, he often showed visitors a tiny, three-room cabin nearly a mile down the river from his comfortable home. The ramshackle house, he claimed, was where he was born.

"Why, Lyndon," his mother said after hearing one of his claims, "you know you were born in a much better house closer to town which has been torn down." Lyndon replied, "I know, Mama, but everybody has to have a birthplace."

In his mature years, Lyndon enjoyed giving the impression that he, like Abraham Lincoln, had been born in a cabin in the wilderness. Actually, the Johnson family was already well known in central Texas years before Lyndon was born. About thirteen miles from the family farm is Johnson City, which during Lyndon's youth was a town of about three hundred residents. Johnson City was named after Lyndon's grandfather, Sam Ealy Johnson, Sr. Following the Civil War, Sam Senior and his brother had settled in the area to raise cattle.

When Lyndon was six years old, his parents decided to move into a house in Johnson City, although they still kept the ranch. In 1914, Johnson City was hardly modern. There were no paved roads, electricity, or gas lines. A few homes had telephones, and a few early automobiles chugged noisily along the bumpy roads. For a time, Sam Junior tried his hand at the real estate business, with limited success.

For his growing family, life in the village of Johnson City was not too different from life on the ranch. Neither the ranch house nor the house in the village had indoor plumbing or electricity. Both homes were heated by wood stoves and fireplaces. Before long, the family moved back to the ranch, which at least could provide food when the real estate business did not.

Above: Lyndon (center) and his family at the cabin in Pedernales Valley
Below: The Johnson family home in Johnson City, Texas

The Johnson children: Lucia, Josefa, Rebekah, Lyndon, and Sam

There were plenty of chores for Lyndon on the ranch as well as in the village. He soon learned how to organize others to help do the work. As the oldest child, he passed out chores such as feeding the pigs and gathering eggs from the chicken coop to his younger brother and sisters. When it was time to chop and stack firewood, he invited schoolmates over to help, establishing contests to see who could cut and stack the fastest, and then passing out some of Rebekah's cookies to all the volunteers.

Lyndon sometimes rode a donkey to school and, as he grew, his long legs nearly dragged on the ground. Although he seldom carried a book home, his grades were generally excellent. The friends he chose were usually older than himself, and he often went to school wearing a dress shirt and tie, the only student dressed that way.

By the time he was in high school, Lyndon towered over most of his classmates. He had unusually long legs and large ears. Already he had a particularly strong interest in politics and government. When a trial was in session at the courthouse in Johnson City, he once asked his high school civics teacher to let the class observe the proceedings. Although the teacher at first objected, his persuasive student soon talked him into agreeing. Lyndon and a few of his classmates also found a local resident who got copies of the *Congressional Record*, the official report of activities in the U.S. Congress. He read carefully many editions of the *Congressional Record*.

The little high school Lyndon attended in Johnson City offered classes only through the eleventh grade, although a twelfth grade was taught in most other high schools. He was elected president of the eleventh grade class, which included five other students in addition to himself. He graduated in May 1924 at the age of fifteen, already six feet three inches tall. His classmates boasted that he was the youngest graduate in the history of the school and predicted that he would become governor of Texas.

In 1924, the United States was in the midst of a decade often called the "Roaring Twenties." For much of America it was an era of prosperity. World War I had ended in 1918, and the stock market crash leading to the Great Depression was still years away. Jobs were generally easy to find. By the millions, Americans were buying automobiles, talking on the telephone, and listening to jazz music on radios and phonographs. In the hill country of central Texas, things were much different.

"When I finished high school in 1924 there wasn't anything going," Johnson said in a speech after he had left the presidency. "No work at all in Johnson City, nowhere around here. My father finally got me kind of a job—not that I wasn't grateful for it—down in Robstown, Texas, which is south of Houston. It was a clerical job and didn't pay much and wasn't in any way the kind of job I had in mind, sitting behind a desk all day. I don't think I stayed there more than a few weeks and then I quit or got fired maybe. I don't remember."

Against the advice of both his parents, especially his father, Lyndon and four or five of his friends packed food and a few belongings into a Model T Ford and drove to California. It was a long trip, but the friends managed to get to San Bernardino, California, by the middle of July 1925, eight or ten days after they had begun.

"That was the first time I went on a diet," Lyndon told one of his biographers years later. "Nothing to eat was the principal item on my food chart. Up and down the coast I tramped, washing dishes, waiting on tables, doing farmwork when it was available, and always growing thinner and more homesick."

He went on to say that, near starvation, he left California and hitchhiked all the way back to Texas, in a very weak condition.

In reality, Lyndon was driven home by a man named Thomas Martin, who helped him during his early political career and certainly gave him some food along the way. "Lyndon often remembered things as being worse than they were," his brother Sam Houston Johnson once said.

Lyndon in 1926
at the age
of eighteen

There is no denying that Lyndon faced a difficult time back in Texas. He found a job driving a mule-powered road-building machine near the family ranch; but the work was exhausting, and Johnson found it hard to endure the cold winter weather. At home, Rebekah urged him to enter Southwest Texas State Teachers College. The campus at San Marcos was only about forty miles from Johnson City. "I'd just gone through January on the road gang," Lyndon said years later, "and it was cold weather, very cold. At that moment the prospect of going to school in the spring had some appeal to me."

Lyndon arrived on the San Marcos campus in February 1927 with a little money he had saved from his road work and $75 he had borrowed from a local banker. His first experience with college was a shock: he discovered he might not be allowed to enroll.

Lyndon (right) with two of his fellow debaters

Because the high school in Johnson City taught classes only through the eleventh grade, it was not accredited by the state of Texas. In order to enter Southwest Texas State Teachers College, he would have to take a crash course at the school and pass a difficult exam. A few days before the test, Rebekah came to the campus and tutored her son in the areas in which he was weak, particularly plane geometry. When he took the entrance exam, he scored a seventy in plane geometry, the minimum passing grade. It hadn't been easy, but at last he enrolled in college.

At college, Lyndon became a champion debater, winning contest after contest although he rarely studied hard preparing for them. Instead, he listened to the things

Johnson (middle row, center) with his students at Cotulla

others said and then learned to focus on the weak points of every argument. He never lost a debate. He also worked on the school newspaper, several times as editor-in-chief, and held a wide variety of part-time jobs.

Despite all the hard work, Lyndon had to take nine months off, starting in the summer of 1928, to earn more money. Because he had completed two years of college, he was allowed to teach elementary school in Texas. In the little town of Cotulla south of San Antonio, he taught English and other subjects to Mexican-American children, most of whom spoke Spanish at home. Although he was offered another contract at the little school, in June 1929 he returned to San Marcos to complete his college education.

Left: Johnson with three other teachers at the Cotulla elementary school

Below: The entire faculty of the Cotulla school in 1928. Lyndon is sitting in front on the right.

Cotulla
Faculty

71

Throughout his final two years of formal schooling, Lyndon worked exceptionally hard. During his senior year, he taught two courses in freshman government, served as secretary to the college president, and managed to carry seven courses—more than the college officially allowed students to take. "I had a date every night, too," he once bragged. "Never got more than three or four hours' sleep." He lived and worked with that intense energy throughout his adult life.

Lyndon Johnson graduated from Southwest Texas State Teachers College with a bachelor of science degree in August 1930. He attained a four-year degree even though he had spent less than four years at college and, during that period, took off nine months to teach elementary school. He was rightfully proud of his achievement but could still joke about his alma mater. When he was president, he had a White House dinner party for the prime minister of Canada, which a number of top U.S. government officials attended. During the dinner, he offered a toast, saying: "It is gratifying to see at this table tonight the most superbly educated men in the world, for in this room there are three Rhodes scholars, four graduates of Harvard, three of Yale, and one from Southwest Texas State Teachers College."

When Lyndon graduated, America's Great Depression was just beginning. Jobs were hard to find, and many teachers were being laid off. Although he managed to get a job teaching school in the little town of Pearsall, his teaching career was brief. The world of politics was about to open up to him.

# Chapter 3

# Up the Political Ladder

Even in the first year of America's Great Depression—1930—many people, including college-educated teachers, discovered that jobs were scarce and hard to keep. In the midst of rising unemployment, Lyndon managed to find not one job but two in his home state. He became principal of a little school in Pearsall; but after serving only a month, he accepted a job at Sam Houston High School in Houston, where his uncle taught history. As the new public-speaking teacher at the high school, Lyndon managed the debate team.

He was shocked to learn that the team had lost its debates for four years in a row to a neighboring school. Lyndon vowed to turn things around—and he certainly did! Of the 67 debates held with Lyndon Johnson as the debating coach, Sam Houston High School won 66, losing only at the Texas state championship. During that contest, his team was unlucky enough to have to debate in favor of the proposition: "Resolved, that the jury system should be abolished."

Opposite page: Johnson in the House
of Representatives in the 1930s

**The Sam Houston High School Debate Team of 1931**

"I just almost cried when we drew the affirmative, and we lost by just one vote, three to two," Lyndon said years later. Despite the loss, the Houston school board was impressed by the young debate teacher. While many other teachers in the area were getting pay cuts, Lyndon Johnson's salary was increased by $100 a year.

In the fall of 1931, he returned to Sam Houston High School, but his teaching career ended suddenly when a newly elected congressman from Texas offered him a job as a personal secretary. The new congressman was Richard Kleberg. Kleberg's father was one of the owners of the million-acre King Ranch in Texas, the largest ranch and private landholding in the world. Lyndon often liked to point out that the entire state of Connecticut could fit easily inside the King Ranch.

Two unemployed New Yorkers selling apples during the Great Depression

Congressman Kleberg and his new personal secretary traveled by train from Texas to Washington, D.C. For a few days, Lyndon stayed at the posh Mayflower Hotel as a guest of the congressman. Then he moved to the much more modest Dodge Hotel, where many congressional aides lived. Until recently, the Dodge had been a hotel for women. Now that the Depression had started, the bottom two floors were opened to men. Lyndon and a roommate shared a small room at the Dodge for just $20 a month per person.

The young Texan soon discovered that working for Congressman Kleberg was a demanding job. The congressman seemed to spend much of his time at the Burning Tree Golf Course in nearby Maryland. Lyndon was frequently left alone to pass out work to other members of the congressman's staff, to answer letters and telephone calls, and to speak with other congressmen and their secretaries.

Johnson in
Washington in 1931
when he was personal
secretary to
Congressman Kleberg

He also began to show other politicians in Washington the
energy for which he soon became famous. He was always
at the office by 7:00 or 7:30 in the morning and normally
worked late into the night. Lyndon was as demanding of
others as he was of himself. He insisted that people for
whom the congressman had found jobs report to him in
the evening to do more work. He managed Richard
Kleberg's office so thoroughly that he even wrote personal
letters to the congressman's mother.

Secretary Johnson joined, and soon took over, an
organization of congressional secretaries known as the Little Congress, which met in one of the hearing rooms in the
House of Representatives. After attending a few of the
meetings and seeing that there were relatively few people
there, he encouraged other secretaries to join. When they

The picture of Lady Bird that Johnson kept in his office as president

did, they soon voted for him as speaker, the top office in the Little Congress. The energetic speaker of the Little Congress managed to find well-known senators and congressmen willing to talk to the group.

During the four years Lyndon worked as a congressional secretary, he made occasional trips back to Texas. On one of these trips, in September 1934, he met a young woman named Claudia Alta Taylor in Austin. Claudia, the daughter of a wealthy Texas landowner, had been known by the nickname Lady Bird, or simply Bird, since she was a baby. Apparently, Lyndon decided to marry her almost immediately. "I don't think Bird ever had a chance to say no—if she wanted to," said a family friend about the whirlwind romance.

**Lyndon and Lady Bird on their honeymoon in Mexico**

Lyndon drove back to Texas so that he and Lady Bird could be married on November 17, 1934, about a month after they had met. Money was hard to come by during the Depression years, even for a congressman's secretary; Lady Bird's wedding ring was purchased at a Sears & Roebuck department store by a friend of Lyndon's for $2.50. Over the years, the couple had two daughters, Lynda Bird and Luci Baines. Counting Lady Bird's nickname, all four members of the family had the initials LBJ.

Lady Bird moved with her new husband to Washington, where they lived in several different apartments in the northwest section of the city while Lyndon continued working as a congressional secretary. He enrolled at Georgetown Law School, where he attended night classes for a while; but his career in law was short-lived. In August 1935, he was offered a new job that would send him back to Texas.

At the time, America was suffering through the darkest years of the Great Depression. Many people were without jobs, homes, decent clothes, and even enough food to eat. America's Democratic president, Franklin Roosevelt, was elected in a popular landslide in 1932 after promising to help the approximately fourteen million Americans who were out of work at the time. In a vast legislative program called the New Deal, Roosevelt developed and guided through Congress many laws designed to help the nation's poor people. He also set up a number of major programs by Executive Order, in other words, on the authority of the president without the approval of Congress.

On June 26, 1935, President Roosevelt established the National Youth Administration (NYA) by Executive Order. The purpose of the program was to provide part-time employment for many of the country's five million unemployed young people. The president hoped that the jobs created would help many underprivileged youngsters continue their education. Lyndon Johnson was named director of the Texas NYA on July 26. Still a month away from his twenty-seventh birthday, Lyndon was the youngest NYA state director in the nation.

**Congressman Johnson at the White House**

Lyndon soon had his program in position and was working wonders while other state directors were still looking for office furniture. He flew all around the huge state of Texas meeting city mayors to enlist their help in his project. He stretched his limited budget to the maximum, at one point providing help to about 47,000 Texas youths. On Sundays, he called in his far-flung district directors to Austin for staff meetings. The Sunday meetings, of course, gave his district directors the freedom to work full-time in their home territories from Monday through Saturday. The president's wife, Eleanor Roosevelt, made several trips to Austin to meet the director of the increasingly famous Texas program.

Johnson in
the House of
Representatives

Although his work with the Texas NYA was astonish-
ing, Lyndon held his position for only eighteen months.
On February 22, 1937, the U.S. congressman from Lyndon's Texas district, a man named James P. Buchanan,
died following a heart attack. A Texas senator urged Lyndon to run for the vacated congressional seat. Lyndon soon
quit his job to enter the race, competing against eight
other candidates.

Early in the campaign, Lyndon decided to throw his
political fortunes completely behind President Roosevelt's
programs, stating that he backed every one of the president's beliefs. Among them was a controversial idea, called
the Supreme Court-packing plan. The plan would add
more justices to the U.S. Supreme Court to overcome the
votes of the justices opposed to some New Deal legislation.

Although the majority of Americans were against the court-packing plan, candidate Johnson gave it his full support, calling it "the unpacking plan." He referred to the other candidates, who generally supported Roosevelt with some reservations, as the "Eight in the Dark," devoted to "trembling, fear, and reaction."

Just ten days before the April 10 election, Johnson entered an Austin hospital to have his appendix removed. He was still recuperating in a hospital bed when he learned that he had won the election, with twice as many votes as his closest rival. At the age of twenty-eight, Lyndon Johnson was elected to the U.S. House of Representatives.

President Roosevelt was pleased by the newspaper reports he read of the young congressman-elect from Texas who had so enthusiastically backed his New Deal programs. By an odd coincidence, the president was scheduled to take a fishing trip aboard the presidential yacht in the Gulf of Mexico just off the Texas coast the next month. It gave Roosevelt an early opportunity to meet the young man who had praised him so wholeheartedly.

President Roosevelt and Congressman-Elect Johnson met on the island city of Galveston on May 11, 1937. Roosevelt, who had just caught a 77-pound fish, congratulated the congressman on his victory. The congressman, in turn, congratulated the president on his fine catch, saying that he, too, enjoyed fishing. In reality, fishing was much too slow a sport for the energetic Texan. Roosevelt enjoyed Johnson's company and invited him to travel on the presidential train that would soon be traveling eastward through Texas on the way back to Washington, D.C.

President Roosevelt and Congressman Johnson in Galveston, Texas, in May 1937, while Roosevelt was on a fishing trip

Johnson boarded the train and traveled a short distance with Roosevelt. Even though Johnson was a guest of the president, the conductor asked him to pay for a ticket to Fort Worth, which took nearly all the money he had. "I paid the conductor," the congressman told a reporter for the *Chicago Tribune*, who was also traveling on the train, "but I want to know if I did right. After all, the President invited me aboard."

"You did," the reporter answered. "And let this be a profitable lesson to you. The president is very generous with everybody's money but his own." There can be little doubt how profitable the presidential visit was for the young congressman's career, however. By the time he arrived back in Washington, Lyndon Johnson was already becoming known as the president's protégé, a freshman congressman with a very powerful friend.

Johnson campaigning for the Senate in 1941

In the House of Representatives, Johnson worked hard for his Texas constituents. He brought a number of major public works to Texas, including a large dam and a massive project to bring electricity to rural areas of the state. During these years when the events leading to World War II were building in Europe, Johnson's record on military bills was mixed. However, he seldom missed a chance to help secure military bases and military money for Texas. With the support of President Roosevelt, he quickly became one of the most influential members of the House.

In April 1941, Congressman Johnson stood on the steps of the White House and announced to reporters that he had decided to run for the U.S. Senate. During the campaign, he made a pledge to Texans increasingly concerned about the prospects of war. If America were forced to enter the conflict, he promised, and "my vote must be cast to send your boy to war, that day Lyndon Johnson will leave his seat in Congress to go with him."

Lieutenant Commander Lyndon Johnson in his navy uniform. When he was president, Johnson said he could not remember what he was doing on December 7, 1941, the day the Japanese bombed Pearl Harbor.

Lyndon Johnson lost the election—the only defeat he ever suffered—by a mere 1,311 votes out of more than half a million cast. Even though he lost, he soon had a chance to make good on his campaign promise. Five months after the election, Japanese airplanes bombed Pearl Harbor in Hawaii. America was going to war, and so was Lyndon Johnson.

# Chapter 4

# Soldier, Senator, Super Senator, Vice-President

Unsuccessful in his first bid for the U.S. Senate in 1941, Lyndon Johnson still had his seat in the House of Representatives. On December 8, 1941, one day after the attack on Pearl Harbor, the U.S. Congress declared war on Japan. Immediately after he voted in favor of the war resolution, Congressman Johnson—for some years a member of the U.S. Naval Reserve—requested active duty for himself from navy officials. He was in uniform the next day, the first member of the House of Representatives to join any of the armed forces during the war.

He was assigned to San Francisco but soon appealed to President Roosevelt for more active duty. By May 1942, he was on an island near Australia assessing U.S. military strength in the Pacific for the president. By June 9, Lieutenant Commander Lyndon Johnson found all the war action he could want and still live to tell about it.

Opposite page: Senator Johnson
at the LBJ Ranch in July 1960

While flying in a B-26 bomber group sent to destroy a Japanese airfield, his airplane developed engine trouble and quickly fell behind the other aircraft. A group of six or eight Japanese Zeros (fighter planes) spotted the crippled bomber and swooped down to attack it. The B-26 pilot put his aircraft into a sudden dive hoping to reach a cloud for cover, and Johnson was tossed around violently.

The speedy Zeros followed the B-26 into the low-altitude cloud and peppered the plane with machine gun fire. Since the Zeros were much faster than the heavy B-26, the Americans knew they had little chance of out-running them. Instead, the pilot executed a brilliant maneuver by flying low above the ocean waves, at times only ten or twenty feet above the water, which made it impossible for the Zeros to attack from below. The crew concentrated all the bomber's fire power above and behind the craft, and held off the Zeros until the B-26 was out of the fighters' range. The airplane, heavily damaged but its crew intact, managed to get back to its base on the island of New Guinea. For his "marked coolness in spite of the hazard involved," Lieutenant Commander Johnson was awarded the Silver Star Medal.

Before the end of the same month, he fell seriously ill with pneumonia and was hospitalized for twelve days. He returned to the United States nearly thirty pounds lighter than when he had left. By that time, President Roosevelt already had ordered all senators and congressmen fighting in the war to come back to the United States to serve in Congress. For Lyndon Johnson and his congressional counterparts, the fighting war was over.

Johnson in New Guinea during the war, with Brigadier General Martin Scanlon and General Ralph Royce

Back in the Congress, Johnson worked on a number of laws designed to help the American war effort. When the Japanese surrendered to end World War II, Johnson was already a working member of the Postwar Military Policy Committee and later a member of the new Joint Committee on Atomic Energy.

By 1948, Congressman Johnson had served five terms in the U.S. House of Representatives. The man who once said that life ended at age forty was now facing that milestone. He and Lady Bird now had two daughters, one-year-old Luci Baines and four-year-old Lynda Bird. For a time, he considered leaving politics in the hope of earning more money in another profession. During a May trip to Austin, the capital of Texas, a number of his friends urged him to run for the U.S. Senate once again.

**The Johnson family in January 1965, right before Lyndon's inauguration: Lynda Bird (left), Lyndon, Luci Baines (right), and Lady Bird**

**The proud grandfather balances his week-old grandson, Patrick Lyndon, on his knee at the Johnson ranch in Johnson City, Texas, July 1967.**

**Johnson after winning the Senate nomination**

To win the Democratic Party's nomination to run for the Senate, Johnson had to defeat a popular Democratic politician named Coke Stevenson, who had recently retired as the governor of Texas. In solidly Democratic Texas of the late 1940s, whoever won the Democratic nomination was almost bound to win the election.

Lyndon Johnson began his campaign for the U.S. Senate by adopting the goals of "preparedness, peace, and progress." Since World War II had ended just three years earlier, the desire of all Americans, including Texans, for peace and military preparedness was strong. To improve the economy of Texas and the U.S., Johnson called for a number of measures. These included price supports for farmers and higher salaries for teachers, large public projects to blacktop roads and bring electricity to rural areas of Texas, and a number of proposals for fair working laws and public health and welfare measures.

The Johnson City Flying Windmill on the campaign trail

What captured Texas voters' attention was not so much what Johnson said during the campaign—or even how he said it. It was his method of transportation that caused the greatest stir. Texas is a huge state, at that time the largest in the U.S. (Alaska, which joined the Union in 1958, is now the largest.) In order to visit each of the 254 counties in the state, Johnson rode aboard a helicopter, an aircraft perfected less than a decade earlier. Many residents of Texas had never seen a helicopter, and the sight of the senatorial candidate arriving in one was a great novelty. The candidate himself was frequently heard on local radio stations announcing that he would be arriving soon in the "Johnson City Flying Windmill," the name he gave to his helicopter.

In his Austin home, Johnson waits for vote counts in the Democratic primary.

The nearly 1,200,000 votes cast for senator in the Texas Democratic primary were divided among eleven candidates. None received a majority of the votes. To choose a Democratic candidate for the Senate, Texas held a runoff election between the two top candidates—Coke Stevenson and Lyndon Johnson. The election was extraordinarily close. After several bitter court battles, it was determined that Lyndon had won the election by a total of eighty-seven votes out of nearly a million cast.

Although he won the Democratic nomination by a whisker, his race against the Republican candidate was no contest. While Democratic President Harry Truman recorded a stunning upset over his highly favored Republican opponent, Lyndon Johnson walked into the U.S. Senate, receiving twice as many votes as his Republican challenger, without making a single campaign speech. It wasn't necessary in strongly Democratic Texas.

Johnson the campaigner

Senator Johnson reached the floor of the U.S. Senate already running. From his first day, he devoted himself to the business of the Senate. "He is entirely preoccupied with the science of politics," a reporter wrote of him a few years after the election. "He refused to be trapped into thinking about or discussing sports, literature, the stage, the movies, or anything else in the world of recreation." Instead, he worked from dawn to dusk on legislative issues.

More than anyone else in recent history, Senator Johnson knew that the way to get legislation passed on Capitol Hill was to "wheel and deal" with people. When he met with his colleagues to discuss an upcoming vote, he used his energetic style and every means of persuasion he could muster to get them on his side. He soon developed what became known as the "Johnson Treatment" when trying to get other senators to vote his way.

**Senator Johnson at a news conference in his office**

The Treatment involved fast talking, often laced with colorful and sometimes obscene language. As he was making a point, he would frequently jab the listener in the chest with a finger or put his arms around him to show the warm support he was seeking. One writer called the Treatment "an incredibly potent mixture of persuasion, badgering, flattery, threats, reminders of past favors and future advantages." Once, Senator Hubert Humphrey, talking with friends after he had received the Johnson Treatment, raised one of his trouser legs to reveal a number of bruises on his shin. According to Humphrey, Senator Johnson had kicked him there as he shouted, "Get going now!"

General Eisenhower (before he was president) and Senator Johnson at a
hearing about drafting eighteen-year-olds

Johnson's powers of persuasion were noticed by the
other Democratic senators in Congress. They soon
appointed him the party "whip," the man responsible for
making sure that other Democratic senators followed the
party philosophy and were in attendance for important
votes. In January 1953, shortly after Dwight Eisenhower
was elected president of the United States, Democratic
senators voted for Lyndon Johnson as minority leader of
the Senate. The following year, Senator Johnson, up for
reelection for the first time, won easily. During the same
election, the Democrats took over control of the Senate.
Lyndon Johnson, at the age of forty-five, was now Senate
majority leader, one of the most important political posi-
tions in the nation. Some people felt he was the second
most powerful politician in America, after Eisenhower.

Although Senate Majority Leader Johnson and President Eisenhower were in different political parties, Johnson tried hard to work with, rather than against, the popular Republican president. The middle years of the 1950s were enjoyable times for politicians and ordinary citizens.

The Korean War, a small but bloody conflict fought in Asia, had been waged under both President Truman and President Eisenhower, but it ended with a truce in 1953. By the following year, America was at peace and the economy was booming. Many American families were beginning to find that they had enough money to buy second cars and new homes in the suburbs. When President Eisenhower suggested that America adopt a minimum wage law, guaranteeing that most employees would make at least ninety cents an hour, Senate Majority Leader Johnson threw his full weight behind the proposal. Under Johnson's leadership, America's new minimum wage was established at one dollar per hour.

On many other issues, Senator Johnson helped President Eisenhower pass needed legislation in Congress. On one major issue, however, he was sharply critical of the president. During the spring of 1954, French troops were fighting Communist soldiers in the Asian country of Vietnam (then known as French Indochina). When it appeared that the French were losing the war, President Eisenhower considered sending American troops into the battle. Johnson did not want America to act alone; and when the British refused to send troops as well, the plan was abandoned. For Lyndon Johnson and America, however, the story of Vietnam was far from over.

Johnson and fellow senators celebrate the passage of the 1957 civil rights law.

On July 2, 1955, Senator Johnson suffered a heart attack. Although the attack was terribly painful and life-threatening, he survived and managed to return to the Senate about six months later. His energy seemed undiminished. By the following year, 1957, he led the fight for the first American civil rights law in nearly a century. Three years later, in 1960, he guided a second civil rights bill through the Senate, which guaranteed to many blacks the right to register to vote.

By the beginning of the 1960s, many people believed that Senator Johnson had the experience and ability to become president of the United States. His powers of persuasion had been proven in the U.S. Senate. His ability to compromise between the sometimes conflicting views of northerners and southerners had been shown by his work on two major civil rights laws. After the Russians launched *Sputnik,* the world's first artificial satellite, he worked to get America into the space race.

Johnson meets with Kennedy in Hyannis Port, Massachusetts

Although many people thought he should run for president, Senator Johnson did not enter any of the primary elections for the 1960 presidential race. Even so, at the Democratic nominating convention that same year, a significant number of delegates still voted for him. However, more delegates voted for John F. Kennedy, the handsome young senator from Massachusetts, who won the Democratic nomination on the first ballot. Although some delegates thought that Johnson and Kennedy were political enemies, the young nominee surprised the convention by announcing that he would like to have Lyndon Johnson as his vice-presidential running mate. A number of Senator Johnson's closest friends were equally amazed when Lyndon accepted the vice-presidency, a role that was basically an assistant to the president. John Kennedy realized what a

Johnson accepts the Democratic vice-presidential nomination in Los Angeles, July 1960.

number of delegates did not: Lyndon Johnson, well liked in the southern states, could help the Democrats win the election against Republican Richard Nixon.

John Kennedy was right. In a very close election, the Democrats won in November. The two pivotal states in the victory were Illinois and Texas, the latter Lyndon Johnson's home state. On the same day that the American people chose Lyndon Johnson as the new vice-president of the United States, the voters of Texas reelected him to the U.S. Senate. On January 3, 1961, he was sworn in for his third term as a U.S. senator from Texas. Three minutes later, he resigned. As he often had done in the past, Senator Johnson decided to follow a higher calling. He took the oath of office for vice-president on January 20, 1961.

President Kennedy meets with his cabinet members.

Kennedy brought many of the brightest thinkers in the nation to Washington when he became president. Vice-President Johnson, a graduate of Southwest Texas State Teachers College, seemed to feel he couldn't keep up with some of them. "You should see all the brains the president has rounded up in his cabinet and White House staff," he said to his old Texas friend, Speaker of the House Sam Rayburn. "Why, those that haven't graduated from Harvard are Ph.D.s—and some are both."

"Yes, Lyndon," Sam Rayburn reportedly answered, "but I wish just one of them had run for sheriff in his home county." Sam Rayburn's point was clear. Although Vice-President Johnson did not have the expensive Ivy League education many of the president's top advisers enjoyed, he had the political experience, and the respect of American voters, to make up for it.

Vice-President Johnson reports to Kennedy about his September 1963 European tour.

The responsibilities of the vice-president of the United States are much lighter than those of the president, but Lyndon Johnson was not one to take things easy. He filled his three-year term with cabinet meetings, trips abroad, meetings of the National Aeronautics and Space Council (of which he was the chairman), and the vice-president's usual responsibilities as president of the Senate.

His energetic career as vice-president was cut short, however, on November 22, 1963. Just as the campaign season for the 1964 elections was about to get under way, he and President Kennedy made their tragic visit to Dallas, Texas. Three hours after arriving, Lyndon Johnson left Dallas as the new president of a stunned America.

**President Lyndon B. Johnson**

# Chapter 5

# The Thirty-Sixth President

President Lyndon Johnson did what he could to ease the pain and share the sorrow of a nation stricken by John F. Kennedy's assassination. Five days after the tragedy, he addressed a joint session of Congress. Near the beginning of his speech, he said, "All I have I would have given gladly not to be standing here today." He referred to the slain president's hopes for worldwide freedom, prosperity, peace, and civil rights, and recalled the fact that Kennedy had once said: "Let us begin."

The new president made it clear that he intended to follow John Kennedy's program. "I would say to all my fellow Americans," he said, "let us continue." He added that he hoped President Kennedy could be honored by a swift passage of a new civil rights law that the late president had worked for. "We have talked long enough in this country about equal rights. We have talked for one hundred years or more. It is time now to write the next chapter, and to write it in the books of law."

To help ensure a smooth transition to the new administration, President Johnson kept all of John Kennedy's cabinet members on his own cabinet staff. While the new president seemed determined to carry on the policies of the fallen president, Lyndon Johnson also brought a new dimension to his office. Few American presidents, certainly none in modern times, have understood the U.S. Congress as thoroughly as Lyndon Johnson. A powerful member of both houses, especially the Senate, he had developed the Johnson Treatment into an effective tool of political persuasion. From the White House, he was able to bend Congress to his wishes with great success.

Lyndon Johnson was also the first southern president since Andrew Johnson, who had held the office a century earlier. By using his skills at handling congressmen, and winning over some of the southern politicians reluctant to support additional civil rights legislation, Johnson was able to enact some of the most important civil rights laws in American history. The Civil Rights Act of 1964 was particularly significant. The law banned discrimination in most public places, helped more minority members gain the right to vote, hastened school desegregation, and allowed the federal government to withhold funds from any states, institutions, agencies, and companies that practiced discrimination.

By the middle of 1964, the year he faced his first election for the presidency, Johnson also began speaking of his dream for a "Great Society." In many respects, President Johnson's Great Society had the same goals as those President Kennedy sought. Because Johnson was a master at

**Sioux Indian children in a Head Start program in South Dakota**

congressional politics, he was able to get laws passed quickly that were aimed at improving the quality of life in America, especially for minority groups and the poor. Starting with the Economic Opportunity Act of 1964, Congress passed a series of laws creating federal programs designed to improve the health, education, employment, and living standards of many underprivileged Americans. A few of these programs were the Neighborhood Youth Corps, Head Start, Job Corps, VISTA, and Medicare.

Despite his energetic approach to national matters, President Johnson tended to act cautiously in foreign affairs. Soon after John Kennedy's assassination, Cuba's Fidel Castro demanded that the U.S. close its Guantánamo naval base on the island nation. To underscore his demand, Castro had water supplies to the base turned off. Rather than risk an international incident, the president told naval officials to find a way to get their own water. When the president threatened to fire Cuban workers at the base and seized a number of Cuban fishing boats that had strayed into American waters, Castro eventually turned the water back on. President Johnson also avoided a dangerous situation in Panama, when he negotiated a new agreement over the Panama Canal after the government of Panama had severed relations with the United States.

The president at first proceeded cautiously as well in the growing Vietnam War, a conflict that eventually over-shadowed his entire presidency and seriously divided American public opinion. Since 1950 the American government had pledged "economic and military" assistance to the Asian area. At the end of President Eisenhower's second term of office in 1961, slightly fewer than a thousand American troops were in the country of South Vietnam helping the government fight Communist soldiers. By the end of President Kennedy's administration, the number of American troops in Vietnam had risen to about 25,000. In the first year of Johnson's presidency, he did little to alter the American presence in Southeast Asia. But by 1964, the war in Vietnam had become a campaign issue in that year's presidential election.

Senator Barry
Goldwater
of Arizona

The race quickly shaped up as a contest between conservatives and liberals. At the Republican National Convention, the Republicans nominated Senator Barry Goldwater of Arizona as their choice for president of the United States. The Democrats nominated Lyndon Johnson, who would now face his first presidential race.

Barry Goldwater was a strongly conservative politician, one of only six Republican senators who voted against the Civil Rights Act of 1964. He refused to denounce the radically conservative John Birch Society, stating that "extremism in the defense of liberty is no vice." He also called for a new direction in the war in Vietnam. Goldwater accused President Johnson of following a "no-win" battle plan and suggested that he could end the war quickly. At one point, he told a reporter that he would drop an atomic bomb on Chinese supply lines leading into neighboring North Vietnam, a Communist nation determined to help the rebel soldiers in the south.

**President Johnson and Vice-President Hubert Humphrey**

Many Democrats criticized Goldwater's apparent willingness to risk the start of a nuclear holocaust to win the war in Vietnam. In television and print advertisements, a nuclear explosion was shown above a child holding a flower. The suggestion was clear. President Johnson was a man of peace and restraint. Candidate Goldwater was not. "We don't want our American boys to do the fighting for Asian boys," said candidate Johnson repeatedly.

When election day finally arrived in November 1964, Johnson won a smashing victory. He received 43 million votes to 27 million for Goldwater, the largest popular majority in history. In Congress, many Democratic candidates defeated conservative Republicans, giving the president even greater control over both houses. Johnson was now elected to the presidency and at last had a vice-president, Hubert Humphrey of Minnesota. As the war in Asia grew worse, the president found it increasingly difficult to live up to his reputation as a man of peace.

**A B-57 bomber bombs a suspected Viet Cong storage area in lower South Vietnam.**

In August 1964, several months before the American elections, it was reported that two U.S. naval ships cruising in the Gulf of Tonkin eleven miles from the shore of North Vietnam had been attacked by torpedo boats. In retaliation, Johnson ordered air strikes against several North Vietnamese military bases but stated that "we still seek no wider war."

Soon after the elections, the war began to escalate dramatically. When South Vietnamese Viet Cong soldiers attacked a base at Pleiku early in 1965, the president ordered another bombing attack against North Vietnam. He reasoned that the Viet Cong took their orders from North Vietnam.

During the next three years, as the war continued to widen, the United States dropped more bombs on the relatively small nation of North Vietnam than had been dropped on all enemy targets during World War II. The number of American soldiers fighting in Vietnam eventually reached more than half a million; at the end over 60,000 of them were killed or reported missing in action.

In contrast to the growing conflict in Vietnam, President Johnson continued to press for significant social change at home. One of his greatest achievements came in 1965. That year, he personally appeared before a night session of Congress to appeal for the passage of a new voting rights law, one that would give many blacks the right to vote in areas where that right previously had been denied them. During his plea he said, "It's not just Negroes, but really it's all of us who must overcome the crippling legacy of bigotry and injustice." On August 6, the president proudly signed the Voting Rights Act of 1965. Other important bills he signed the same year included the Medicare program for elderly Americans, a major school aid law, and a bill doubling the amount of money spent to end poverty.

The year 1965 also had its darker side, in both foreign and domestic affairs. In April, news came of an uprising in the Dominican Republic. Believing the rebel soldiers were Communists, President Johnson sent in 20,000 American troops to restore order. Johnson's action provoked a heated debate. Many people argued that the Dominican Republic was led by a cruel dictator and that the uprising was the people's own idea.

A fire truck arrives at a burning building in Watts, August 1965.

At home, racial unrest that had been simmering below the surface for years erupted in violence. In August, six days of rioting in the Watts ghetto of Los Angeles left thirty-five people dead and nearly nine hundred injured. Although Lyndon Johnson did more than most modern presidents for the cause of civil rights, many black people were becoming increasingly frustrated over the slow pace of change in America. The summer of 1965 was the first of several "long, hot summers" of racial unrest during the Johnson administration.

Two U.S. Marines
south of Da Nang,
South Vietnam,
carry a wounded
South Vietnamese
soldier to safety.

Despite an enormous expenditure of money, lives, and materials, America and its South Vietnamese allies seemed unable to win in Vietnam. Many soldiers who returned from the fighting brought with them stories that seemed to suggest Goldwater was right when he accused the president of fighting a "no-win" war. Soldiers, they said, would risk their lives to capture a hill, or a bridge, or a town from the Viet Cong. The next day, they would be ordered away, giving the target back to the Communists. An explanation for this strange way of conducting battles is probably found in President Johnson's determination to wage a "limited war." In time, the grim measure of victory was not land taken but dead bodies found on the ground. Each week, the U.S. Department of Defense issued "body counts," a list of dead enemy soldiers, as well as Americans, as if this measured progress in the war.

An anti-war demonstration at the University of California at Berkeley

Although most Americans seemed to be in favor of the conflict during the early years of Johnson's administration, small but increasing numbers became strongly opposed to it. College students especially, many of them subject to the military draft and the possibility of fighting and dying in Vietnam, tended to be against the war. As the conflict escalated, more of these students, along with some of their teachers, were joining demonstrations calling for an end to the fighting in Vietnam.

Martin Luther King addresses followers in Selma, Alabama, after their 1965
civil rights march on Montgomery, Alabama. Next to King is Andrew Young.

Civil rights leaders like Dr. Martin Luther King, Jr., also
became more disturbed by events in Vietnam. Although
many had given their cautious support to President
Johnson's Great Society and the social reforms it promised,
now they saw the war in Vietnam threatening the progress
of social change. The fears were well founded. The huge
costs of the war required drastic cuts in programs designed
to fight poverty and racial discrimination.

By 1967, a growing minority of congressmen and other
political leaders were adding their voices to those of students and civil rights leaders in criticizing the war. At the
same time, action in Vietnam intensified. On May 19,

**Thurgood Marshall, great-grandson of a slave and first black Supreme Court justice**

American jet planes bombed downtown Hanoi, the capital of North Vietnam, for the first time. In a single week of that same month, a new record for weekly U.S. casualties was set at nearly three thousand. Such news overshadowed the positive side of Johnson's actions. That year LBJ refused to allow America to become involved in a war that broke out between Egypt and Israel in June. In addition, civil rights leaders applauded the president's appointment of the nation's first black Supreme Court justice, Thurgood Marshall. But Vietnam was engulfing Lyndon Johnson's presidency, and good news was becoming increasingly hard to find.

The intelligence ship U.S.S. *Pueblo* before it was seized by North Korea

The following year, 1968, was filled with tragic events both for President Johnson and for the nation. On January 23, the U.S.S. *Pueblo*, a navy spy ship, was captured off North Korea; it would be nearly a year before the crew was freed. A few days later, South Vietnamese Viet Cong soldiers launched a major military offensive, attacking targets across much of South Vietnam. Although U.S. military officials and President Johnson had claimed that the U.S. was winning the war, the Viet Cong demonstrated they could control most of the country. Even the U.S. embassy in South Vietnam's capital city of Saigon was attacked. Although greater numbers of Americans urged the president to get the U.S. out of Vietnam, the war seemed to have no end in sight.

Left: Senator Eugene McCarthy at a fund-raiser. Right: Senator Robert Kennedy

Across the United States, anti-war demonstrations increased dramatically on college campuses and elsewhere. The chant "Hey, hey, LBJ, how many kids did you kill today?" was often heard at rallies demanding peace.

Presidential elections were scheduled for the end of 1968; and, despite the growing unpopularity of the Vietnam War, most people assumed that Lyndon Johnson would be the Democratic party's candidate for president. During the March 12 New Hampshire primary, however, a strongly anti-war Democratic candidate, Senator Eugene McCarthy, gathered a stunning 42 percent of the vote. Four days later, Robert Kennedy, brother of the slain president, announced his candidacy in the race to take the Democratic nomination away from President Johnson.

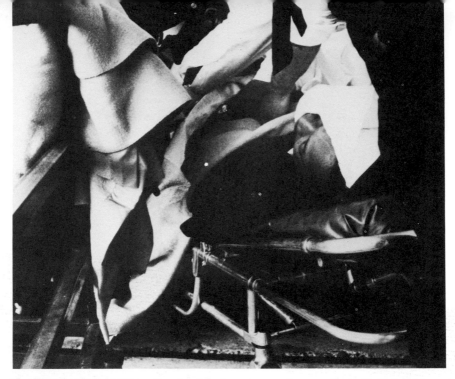

**Dr. Martin Luther King, Jr., is placed on a stretcher on the balcony of his Memphis motel, moments after he was shot.**

Within two weeks of Kennedy's announcement, the president gave in to his critics. In a March 31 televised address he stated that he was restricting the bombing attacks over North Vietnam and asked the North Vietnamese to sit down at a bargaining table to work out a peace plan. At the end of his speech, he startled the nation by announcing he would not run again for president.

On April 4, four days after Johnson's speech, the country was shocked by the news of Dr. Martin Luther King, Jr.'s assassination. The man who had offered blacks their greatest hope for equality had been murdered by a white gunman, James Earl Ray, who was an escaped convict. In anger and despair, blacks rioted in more than 150 American cities. The day following Dr. King's burial in Atlanta, President Johnson signed the important Civil Rights Act of 1968, banning housing discrimination.

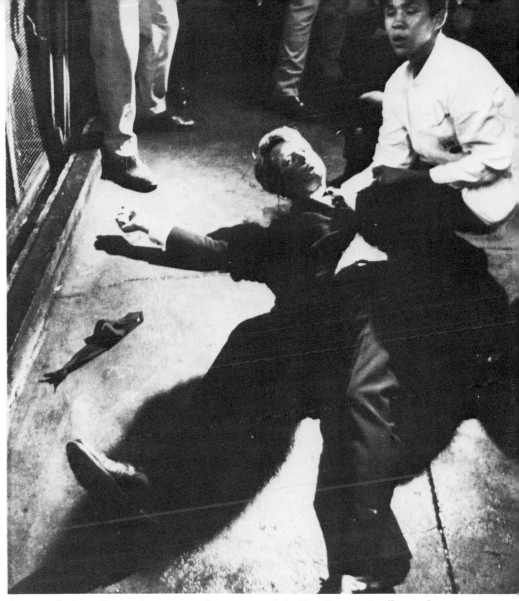

Senator Robert Kennedy, victim of an assassin's bullet, lies on the floor of Los Angeles's Ambassador Hotel, awaiting medical assistance.

For the beleaguered Democratic Party, hope for the future now seemed to lie with Robert Kennedy, who won the all-important California primary on June 5. Late that same evening, he was assassinated by an Arab immigrant named Sirhan Sirhan. Once again the nation mourned one of its young leaders.

**Police and anti-war demonstrators struggle on Michigan Avenue in Chicago during the 1968 Democratic National Convention.**

In August, delegates of the Democratic party — with one leader refusing to run again and two others slain by assassins — came to Chicago to nominate a presidential candidate. Thousands of young protesters gathered to express their displeasure at the nomination of Hubert Humphrey over their candidate, Eugene McCarthy. Unprepared to deal with large, hostile crowds, members of the Chicago police department rushed the demonstrators. The resulting battle between police and the crowds left much of the city in turmoil. In a more peaceful setting, Republicans nominated Richard Nixon as their candidate.

A soldier participating in a mine-sweeping operation in the central highlands of South Vietnam near Bong Son

On October 13, President Johnson announced that all bombing raids over North Vietnam would be halted, hoping that the action would speed up peace negotiations. The war dragged on for another six years, however, eventually ended by the Nixon administration.

Although the presidency of Lyndon Johnson was engulfed by the war in Vietnam, he had made historic contributions to American life. When Johnson stepped down from office in January 1969, he left a legacy of social legislation unmatched by any other modern president. There were also many, many wounds in the nation to heal.

**Above:** At a news conference, LBJ gives an impassioned defense of his Vietnam policies.
**Below:** LBJ greets enlisted men, as General William Westmoreland looks on.

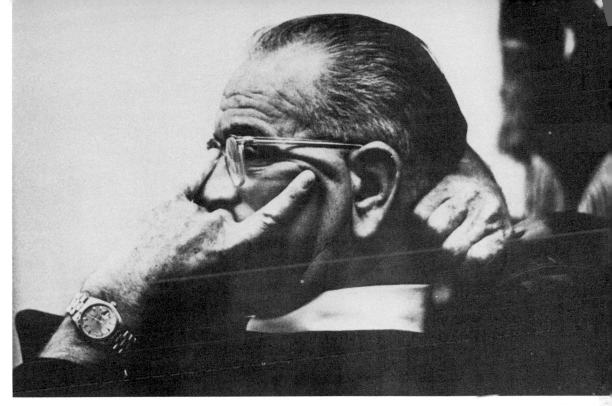

**Above: The president, lost in thought**

**Right: At the LBJ Ranch, Johnson "cuts" a cow from the herd during a press barbecue.**

# Chapter 6

# After the Presidency

Soon after Richard Nixon became the thirty-seventh president of the United States, Lyndon and Lady Bird moved permanently back to their ranch along the Pedernales River in Texas. The ex-president was clearly depressed; and he refused to talk with people, even many close friends, about his presidency. Eventually, though, he found that he could relax a little.

Soon he was able to say about his retirement: "One of the things I enjoyed most was being able to go to bed after the ten o'clock news and sleep until daylight the next morning. I don't remember ever having an experience like that in the five years I was in the White House." The former president began to take an interest in the day-to-day operations of his ranch.

Despite the fact that he suffered some heart pains, and chewed nitroglycerin pills to ease them, he worked not only on the farm but as the chief executive officer of the Texas Broadcasting Company, a local television station he and Lady Bird owned. Periodically, President Nixon would send briefing packets and even cabinet members to fill in the former president on events in Vietnam.

**Former President Johnson chats with President Richard Nixon before they dedicate a California redwood park as "Lady Bird Johnson Grove."**

In the summer of 1970, his "birthplace" cabin not far from the ranch house was taken over by the National Park Service. Visitors to the cabin would often be greeted by the ex-president. Johnson was sometimes seen driving up to the house in a convertible with the top down, calling out to visitors, "You all come on in." Rushing inside with the sightseers, he gleefully pointed out his crib and various other objects that may or may not have been part of his youth. Today, signs at the old cabin by the LBJ Ranch clearly indicate that it is not the president's actual birthplace, despite his repeated stories of a humble birth.

In the spring of 1971, he dedicated the Lyndon Baines Johnson Library and the Lyndon Baines Johnson School of Public Affairs at the University of Texas in Austin. As

Lyndon with Lady Bird
in San Antonio, Texas,
on January 16, 1973,
six days before he died

always, he tried to get as many people as possible to visit both. At a University of Texas football game, he once had a friend ask the public address announcer to invite the entire audience over to his library across the street "for some cool water and to go to the can." Perhaps it is not so difficult to understand why. In that library were all his papers and many of his most personal thoughts—his chance of being remembered in a good light.

LBJ's heritage is not an easy one to understand. Many critics say he handled the Vietnam War poorly. Others believe that his dream of a "Great Society," with the wealth of new laws that were passed trying to achieve it, was an important milestone in American history. Still others claim that his legislation led to many of the problems of our modern welfare state.

Mrs. Johnson receives
the flag that covered
her husband's casket
after his burial on
January 25, 1973.

Lyndon Johnson died on the afternoon of January 22, 1973, in the bedroom of his beloved ranch. Perhaps this complex, sometimes crude, and always hard-driven man summed up his life better than anyone else. In an article he wrote for *Texas Quarterly* magazine in 1959, which was reprinted in *Reader's Digest*, he described himself this way:

"I am a free man, an American, a United States Senator, and a Democrat, in that order. I am also a liberal, a conservative, a consumer, a parent, a voter, and not as young as I used to be nor as old as I expect to be—and I am all those things in no fixed order."

Opposite page: LBJ waves to the crowd
at the 1973 Cotton Bowl in Dallas.

# Chronology of American History

(Shaded area covers events in Lyndon B. Johnson's lifetime.)

**About A.D. 982**—Eric the Red, born in Norway, reaches Greenland in one of the first European voyages to North America.

**About 985**—Eric the Red brings settlers from Iceland to Greenland.

**About 1000**—Leif Ericson (Eric the Red's son) leads what is thought to be the first European expedition to mainland North America; Leif probably lands in Canada.

**1492**—Christopher Columbus, seeking a sea route from Spain to the Far East, discovers the New World.

**1497**—John Cabot reaches Canada in the first English voyage to North America.

**1513**—Ponce de Léon explores Florida in search of the fabled Fountain of Youth.

**1519-1521**—Hernando Cortés of Spain conquers Mexico.

**1534**—French explorers led by Jacques Cartier enter the Gulf of St. Lawrence in Canada.

**1540**—Spanish explorer Francisco Coronado begins exploring the American Southwest, seeking the riches of the mythical Seven Cities of Cibola.

**1565**—St. Augustine, Florida, the first permanent European town in what is now the United States, is founded by the Spanish.

**1607**—Jamestown, Virginia, is founded, the first permanent English town in the present-day U.S.

**1608**—Frenchman Samuel de Champlain founds the village of Quebec, Canada.

**1609**—Henry Hudson explores the eastern coast of present-day U.S. for the Netherlands; the Dutch then claim parts of New York, New Jersey, Delaware, and Connecticut and name the area New Netherland.

**1619**—The English colonies' first shipment of black slaves arrives in Jamestown.

**1620**—English Pilgrims found Massachusetts' first permanent town at Plymouth.

**1621**—Massachusetts Pilgrims and Indians hold the famous first Thanksgiving feast in colonial America.

**1623**—Colonization of New Hampshire is begun by the English.

**1624**—Colonization of present-day New York State is begun by the Dutch at Fort Orange (Albany).

**1625**—The Dutch start building New Amsterdam (now New York City).

**1630**—The town of Boston, Massachusetts, is founded by the English Puritans.

**1633**—Colonization of Connecticut is begun by the English.

**1634**—Colonization of Maryland is begun by the English.

**1636**—Harvard, the colonies' first college, is founded in Massachusetts. Rhode Island colonization begins when Englishman Roger Williams founds Providence.

**1638**—Delaware colonization begins when Swedish people build Fort Christina at present-day Wilmington.

**1640**—Stephen Daye of Cambridge, Massachusetts prints *The Bay Psalm Book*, the first English-language book published in what is now the U.S.

**1643**—Swedish settlers begin colonizing Pennsylvania.

**About 1650**—North Carolina is colonized by Virginia settlers.

**1660**—New Jersey colonization is begun by the Dutch at present-day Jersey City.

**1670**—South Carolina colonization is begun by the English near Charleston.

**1673**—Jacques Marquette and Louis Jolliet explore the upper Mississippi River for France.

1682—Philadelphia, Pennsylvania, is settled. La Salle explores Mississippi River all the way to its mouth in Louisiana and claims the whole Mississippi Valley for France.

1693—College of William and Mary is founded in Williamsburg, Virginia.

1700—Colonial population is about 250,000.

1703—Benjamin Franklin is born in Boston.

1732—George Washington, first president of the U.S., is born in Westmoreland County, Virginia.

1733—James Oglethorpe founds Savannah, Georgia; Georgia is established as the thirteenth colony.

1735—John Adams, second president of the U.S., is born in Braintree, Massachusetts.

1737—William Byrd founds Richmond, Virginia.

1738—British troops are sent to Georgia over border dispute with Spain.

1739—Black insurrection takes place in South Carolina.

1740—English Parliament passes act allowing naturalization of immigrants to American colonies after seven-year residence.

1743—Thomas Jefferson, third president of the U.S., is born in Albemarle County, Virginia. Benjamin Franklin retires at age thirty-seven to devote himself to scientific inquiries and public service.

1744—King George's War begins; France joins war effort against England.

1745—During King George's War, France raids settlements in Maine and New York.

1747—Classes begin at Princeton College in New Jersey.

1748—The Treaty of Aix-la-Chapelle concludes King George's War.

1749—Parliament legally recognizes slavery in colonies and the inauguration of the plantation system in the South. George Washington becomes the surveyor for Culpepper County in Virginia.

1750—Thomas Walker passes through and names Cumberland Gap on his way toward Kentucky region. Colonial population is about 1,200,000.

1751—James Monroe, fourth president of the U.S., is born in Port Conway, Virginia. English Parliament passes Currency Act, banning New England colonies from issuing paper money. George Washington travels to Barbados.

1752—Pennsylvania Hospital, the first general hospital in the colonies, is founded in Philadelphia. Benjamin Franklin uses a kite in a thunderstorm to demonstrate that lightning is a form of electricity.

1753—George Washington delivers command from Virginia Lieutenant Governor Dinwiddie that the French withdraw from the Ohio River Valley; French disregard the demand. Colonial population is about 1,328,000.

1754—French and Indian War begins (extends to Europe as the Seven Years' War). Washington surrenders at Fort Necessity.

1755—French and Indians ambush General Braddock. Washington becomes commander of Virginia troops.

1756—England declares war on France.

1758—James Monroe, fifth president of the U.S., is born in Westmoreland County, Virginia.

1759—Cherokee Indian war begins in southern colonies; hostilities extend to 1761. George Washington marries Martha Dandridge Custis.

1760—George III becomes king of England. Colonial population is about 1,600,000.

1762—England declares war on Spain.

1763—Treaty of Paris concludes the French and Indian War and the Seven Years' War. England gains Canada and most other French lands east of the Mississippi River.

1764—British pass the Sugar Act to gain tax money from the colonists. The issue of taxation without representation is first introduced in Boston. John Adams marries Abigail Smith.

1765—Stamp Act goes into effect in the colonies. Business virtually stops as almost all colonists refuse to use the stamps.

1766—British repeal the Stamp Act.

1767—John Quincy Adams, sixth president of the U.S. and son of second president John Adams, is born in Braintree, Massachusetts. Andrew Jackson, seventh president of the U.S., is born in Waxhaw settlement, South Carolina.

1769—Daniel Boone sights the Kentucky Territory.

1770—In the Boston Massacre, British soldiers kill five colonists and injure six. Townshend Acts are repealed, thus eliminating all duties on imports to the colonies except tea.

1771—Benjamin Franklin begins his autobiography, a work that he will never complete. The North Carolina assembly passes the "Bloody Act," which makes rioters guilty of treason.

1772—Samuel Adams rouses colonists to consider British threats to self-government. Thomas Jefferson marries Martha Wayles Skelton.

1773—English Parliament passes the Tea Act. Colonists dressed as Mohawk Indians board British tea ships and toss 342 casks of tea into the water in what becomes known as the Boston Tea Party. William Henry Harrison is born in Charles City County, Virginia.

1774—British close the port of Boston to punish the city for the Boston Tea Party. First Continental Congress convenes in Philadelphia.

1775—American Revolution begins with battles of Lexington and Concord, Massachusetts. Second Continental Congress opens in Philadelphia. George Washington becomes commander-in-chief of the Continental army.

1776—Declaration of Independence is adopted on July 4.

1777—Congress adopts the American flag with thirteen stars and thirteen stripes. John Adams is sent to France to negotiate peace treaty.

1778—France declares war against Great Britain and becomes U.S. ally.

1779—British surrender to Americans at Vincennes. Thomas Jefferson is elected governor of Virginia. James Madison is elected to the Continental Congress.

1780—Benedict Arnold, first American traitor, defects to the British.

1781—Articles of Confederation go into effect. Cornwallis surrenders to George Washington at Yorktown, ending the American Revolution.

1782—American commissioners, including John Adams, sign peace treaty with British in Paris. Thomas Jefferson's wife, Martha, dies. Martin Van Buren is born in Kinderhook, New York.

1784—Zachary Taylor is born near Barboursville, Virginia.

1785—Congress adopts the dollar as the unit of currency. John Adams is made minister to Great Britain. Thomas Jefferson is appointed minister to France.

1786—Shays' Rebellion begins in Massachusetts.

1787—Constitutional Convention assembles in Philadelphia, with George Washington presiding; U.S. Constitution is adopted. Delaware, New Jersey, and Pennsylvania become states.

1788—Virginia, South Carolina, New York, Connecticut, New Hampshire, Maryland, and Massachusetts become states. U.S. Constitution is ratified. New York City is declared U.S. capital.

1789—Presidential electors elect George Washington and John Adams as first president and vice-president. Thomas Jefferson is appointed secretary of state. North Carolina becomes a state. French Revolution begins.

1790—Supreme Court meets for the first time. Rhode Island becomes a state. First national census in the U.S. counts 3,929,214 persons. John Tyler is born in Charles City County, Virginia.

1791—Vermont enters the Union. U.S. Bill of Rights, the first ten amendments to the Constitution, goes into effect. District of Columbia is established.

1792—Thomas Paine publishes *The Rights of Man.* Kentucky becomes a state. Two political parties are formed in the U.S., Federalist and Republican. Washington is elected to a second term, with Adams as vice-president.

1793—War between France and Britain begins; U.S. declares neutrality. Eli Whitney invents the cotton gin; cotton production and slave labor increase in the South.

1794—Eleventh Amendment to the Constitution is passed, limiting federal courts' power. "Whiskey Rebellion" in Pennsylvania protests federal whiskey tax. James Madison marries Dolley Payne Todd.

1795—George Washington signs the Jay Treaty with Great Britain. Treaty of San Lorenzo, between U.S. and Spain, settles Florida boundary and gives U.S. right to navigate the Mississippi. James Polk is born near Pineville, North Carolina.

1796—Tennessee enters the Union. Washington gives his Farewell Address, refusing a third presidential term. John Adams is elected president and Thomas Jefferson vice-president.

1797—Adams recommends defense measures against possible war with France. Napoleon Bonaparte and his army march against Austrians in Italy. U.S. population is about 4,900,000.

1798—Washington is named commander-in-chief of the U.S. army. Department of the Navy is created. Alien and Sedition Acts are passed. Napoleon's troops invade Egypt and Switzerland.

1799—George Washington dies at Mount Vernon. James Monroe is elected governor of Virginia. French Revolution ends. Napoleon becomes ruler of France.

1800—Thomas Jefferson and Aaron Burr tie for president. U.S. capital is moved from Philadelphia to Washington, D.C. The White House is built as presidents' home. Spain returns Louisiana to France. Millard Fillmore is born in Locke, New York.

1801—After thirty-six ballots, House of Representatives elects Thomas Jefferson president, making Burr vice-president. James Madison is named secretary of state.

1802—Congress abolishes excise taxes. U.S. Military Academy is founded at West Point, New York.

1803—Ohio enters the Union. Louisiana Purchase treaty is signed with France, greatly expanding U.S. territory.

1804—Twelfth Amendment to the Constitution rules that president and vice-president be elected separately. Alexander Hamilton is killed by Vice-President Aaron Burr in a duel. Orleans Territory is established. Napoleon crowns himself emperor of France.

1805—Thomas Jefferson begins his second term as president. Lewis and Clark expedition reaches the Pacific Ocean.

1806—Coinage of silver dollars is stopped; resumes in 1836.

1807—Aaron Burr is acquitted in treason trial. Embargo Act closes U.S. ports to trade.

1808—James Madison is elected president. Congress outlaws importing slaves from Africa.

1810—U.S. population is 7,240,000.

1811—William Henry Harrison defeats Indians at Tippecanoe. Monroe is named secretary of state.

1812—Louisiana becomes a state. U.S. declares war on Britain (War of 1812). James Madison is reelected president. Napoleon invades Russia.

1813—British forces take Fort Niagara and Buffalo, New York.

1814—Francis Scott Key writes "The Star-Spangled Banner." British troops burn much of Washington, D.C., including the White House. Treaty of Ghent ends War of 1812. James Monroe becomes secretary of war.

1815—Napoleon meets his final defeat at Battle of Waterloo.

1816—James Monroe is elected president. Indiana becomes a state.

1817—Mississippi becomes a state. Construction on Erie Canal begins.

1818—Illinois enters the Union. The present thirteen-stripe flag is adopted. Border between U.S. and Canada is agreed upon.

1819—Alabama becomes a state. U.S. purchases Florida from Spain. Thomas Jefferson establishes the University of Virginia.

1820—James Monroe is reelected. In the Missouri Compromise, Maine enters the Union as a free (non-slave) state.

1821—Missouri enters the Union as a slave state. Santa Fe Trail opens the American Southwest. Mexico declares independence from Spain. Napoleon Bonaparte dies.

1822—U.S. recognizes Mexico and Colombia. Liberia in Africa is founded as a home for freed slaves.

1823—Monroe Doctrine closes North and South America to European colonizing or invasion.

1824—House of Representatives elects John Quincy Adams president when none of the four candidates wins a majority in national election. Mexico becomes a republic.

1825—Erie Canal is opened. U.S. population is 11,300,000.

1826—Thomas Jefferson and John Adams both die on July 4, the fiftieth anniversary of the Declaration of Independence.

1828—Andrew Jackson is elected president. Tariff of Abominations is passed, cutting imports.

1829—James Madison attends Virginia's constitutional convention. Slavery is abolished in Mexico.

1830—Indian Removal Act to resettle Indians west of the Mississippi is approved.

1831—James Monroe dies in New York City. James A. Garfield is born in Orange, Ohio. Cyrus McCormick develops his reaper.

1832—Andrew Jackson, nominated by the new Democratic Party, is reelected president.

1833—Britain abolishes slavery in its colonies.

1835—Federal government becomes debt-free for the first time.

1836—Martin Van Buren becomes president. Texas wins independence from Mexico. Arkansas joins the Union. James Madison dies at Montpelier, Virginia.

1837—Michigan enters the Union. U.S. population is 15,900,000.

1840—William Henry Harrison is elected president.

1841—President Harrison dies in Washington, D.C., one month after inauguration. Vice-President John Tyler succeeds him.

1844—James Knox Polk is elected president. Samuel Morse sends first telegraphic message.

1845—Texas and Florida become states. Potato famine in Ireland causes massive emigration from Ireland to U.S. Andrew Jackson dies near Nashville, Tennessee.

1846—Iowa enters the Union. War with Mexico begins.

1847—U.S. captures Mexico City.

1848—Zachary Taylor becomes president. Treaty of Guadalupe Hidalgo ends Mexico-U.S. war. Wisconsin becomes a state.

1849—James Polk dies in Nashville, Tennessee.

1850—President Taylor dies in Washington, D.C.; Vice-President Millard Fillmore succeeds him. California enters the Union, breaking tie between slave and free states.

1852—Franklin Pierce is elected president.

1853—Gadsen Purchase transfers Mexican territory to U.S.

1854—"War for Bleeding Kansas" is fought between slave and free states.

1855—Czar Nicholas I of Russia dies, succeeded by Alexander II.

1856—James Buchanan is elected president. In Massacre of Potawatomi Creek, Kansas-slavers are murdered by free-staters.

1858—Minnesota enters the Union. Theodore Roosevelt is born in New York City.

1859—Oregon becomes a state.

1860—Abraham Lincoln is elected president; South Carolina secedes from the Union in protest.

1861—Arkansas, Tennessee, North Carolina, and Virginia secede. Kansas enters the Union as a free state. Civil War begins.

1862—Union forces capture Fort Henry, Roanoke Island, Fort Donelson, Jacksonville, and New Orleans; Union armies are defeated at the battles of Bull Run and Fredericksburg. Martin Van Buren dies in Kinderhook, New York. John Tyler dies near Charles City, Virginia.

1863—Lincoln issues Emancipation Proclamation: all slaves held in rebelling territories are declared free. West Virginia becomes a state.

1864—Abraham Lincoln is reelected. Nevada becomes a state.

1865—Lincoln is assassinated, succeeded by Andrew Johnson. U.S. Civil War ends on May 26. Thirteenth Amendment abolishes slavery.

1867—Nebraska becomes a state. U.S. buys Alaska from Russia for $7,200,000. Reconstruction Acts are passed.

1868—President Johnson is impeached for violating Tenure of Office Act, but is acquitted by Senate. Ulysses S. Grant is elected president. Fourteenth Amendment prohibits voting discrimination.

1870—Fifteenth Amendment gives blacks the right to vote.

1872—Grant is reelected over Horace Greeley. General Amnesty Act pardons ex-Confederates.

1874—Millard Fillmore dies in Buffalo, New York. Herbert Hoover is born in West Branch, Iowa.

1876—Colorado enters the Union. "Custer's last stand": he and his men are massacred by Sioux Indians at Little Big Horn, Montana.

1877—Rutherford B. Hayes is elected president as all disputed votes are awarded to him.

1880—James A. Garfield is elected president.

1881—President Garfield is assassinated and dies in Elberon, New Jersey. Vice-President Chester A. Arthur succeeds him.

1882—U.S. bans Chinese immigration. Franklin D. Roosevelt is born in Hyde Park, New York.

1886—Statue of Liberty is dedicated.

1888—Benjamin Harrison is elected president.

1889—North Dakota, South Dakota, Washington, and Montana become states.

1890—Dwight D. Eisenhower is born in Denison, Texas. Idaho and Wyoming become states.

1892—Grover Cleveland is elected president.

1896—William McKinley is elected president. Utah becomes a state.

1898—U.S. declares war on Spain over Cuba.

1899—Philippines demand independence from U.S.

1900—McKinley is reelected. Boxer Rebellion against foreigners in China begins.

1901—McKinley is assassinated by anarchist; he is succeeded by Theodore Roosevelt.

1902—U.S. acquires perpetual control over Panama Canal.

1903—Alaskan frontier is settled.

1904—Russian-Japanese War breaks out. Theodore Roosevelt wins presidential election.

1905—Treaty of Portsmouth signed, ending Russian-Japanese War.

1906—U.S. troops occupy Cuba.

1907—President Roosevelt bars all Japanese immigration. Oklahoma enters the Union.

1908—William Howard Taft becomes president. Lyndon B. Johnson is born near Stonewall, Texas.

1909—NAACP is founded under W.E.B. DuBois

1910—China abolishes slavery.

1911—Chinese Revolution begins.

1912—Woodrow Wilson is elected president. Arizona and New Mexico become states.

1913—Federal income tax is introduced in U.S. through the Sixteenth Amendment. Richard Nixon is born in Yorba Linda, California.

1914—World War I begins.

1915—British liner *Lusitania* is sunk by German submarine.

1916—Wilson is reelected president.

1917—U.S. breaks diplomatic relations with Germany. Czar Nicholas of Russia abdicates as revolution begins. U.S. declares war on Austria-Hungary. John F. Kennedy is born in Brookline, Massachusetts.

1918—Wilson proclaims "Fourteen Points" as war aims. On November 11, armistice is signed between Allies and Germany.

1919—Eighteenth Amendment prohibits sale and manufacture of intoxicating liquors. Wilson presides over first League of Nations; wins Nobel Peace Prize. Theodore Roosevelt dies in Oyster Bay, New York.

1920—Nineteenth Amendment (women's suffrage) is passed. Warren Harding is elected president.

1921—Adolf Hitler's stormtroopers begin to terrorize political opponents.

1922—Irish Free State is established. Soviet states form USSR. Benito Mussolini forms Fascist government in Italy.

1923—President Harding dies; he is succeeded by Vice-President Calvin Coolidge.

1924—Coolidge is elected president.

1925—Hitler reorganizes Nazi Party and publishes first volume of *Mein Kampf.*

1926—Fascist youth organizations founded in Germany and Italy. Republic of Lebanon proclaimed.

1927—Stalin becomes Soviet dictator. Economic conference in Geneva attended by fifty-two nations.

1928—Herbert Hoover is elected president. U.S. and many other nations sign Kellogg-Briand pacts to outlaw war.

1929—Stock prices in New York crash on "Black Thursday"; the Great Depression begins.

1930—Bank of U.S. and its many branches close (most significant bank failure of the year).

1931—Emigration from U.S. exceeds immigration for first time as Depression deepens.

1932—Franklin D. Roosevelt wins presidential election in a Democratic landslide.

1933—First concentration camps are erected in Germany. U.S. recognizes USSR and resumes trade. Twenty-First Amendment repeals prohibition.

1934—Severe dust storms hit Plains states. President Roosevelt passes U.S. Social Security Act.

1936—Roosevelt is reelected. Spanish Civil War begins. Hitler and Mussolini form Rome-Berlin Axis.

1937—Roosevelt signs Neutrality Act.

1938—Roosevelt sends appeal to Hitler and Mussolini to settle European problems amicably.

1939—Germany takes over Czechoslovakia and invades Poland, starting World War II.

1940—Roosevelt is reelected for a third term.

1941—Japan bombs Pearl Harbor. U.S. declares war on Japan. Germany and Italy declare war on U.S.; U.S. then declares war on them.

1942—Allies agree not to make separate peace treaties with the enemies. U.S. government transfers more than 100,000 Nisei (Japanese-Americans) from west coast to inland concentration camps.

**1943**—Allied bombings of Germany begin.

**1944**—Roosevelt is reelected for a fourth term. Allied forces invade Normandy on D-Day.

**1945**—President Franklin D. Roosevelt dies in Warm Springs, Georgia; Vice-President Harry S. Truman succeeds him. Mussolini is killed; Hitler commits suicide. Germany surrenders. U.S. drops atomic bomb on Hiroshima; Japan surrenders: end of World War II.

**1946**—U.N. General Assembly holds its first session in London. Peace conference of twenty-one nations is held in Paris.

**1947**—Peace treaties are signed in Paris. "Cold War" is in full swing.

**1948**—U.S. passes Marshall Plan Act, providing $17 billion in aid for Europe. U.S. recognizes new nation of Israel. India and Pakistan become free of British rule. Truman is elected president.

**1949**—Republic of Eire is proclaimed in Dublin. Russia blocks land route access from Western Germany to Berlin; airlift begins. U.S., France, and Britain agree to merge their zones of occupation in West Germany. Apartheid program begins in South Africa.

**1950**—Riots in Johannesburg, South Africa, against apartheid. North Korea invades South Korea. U.N. forces land in South Korea and recapture Seoul.

**1951**—Twenty-Second Amendment limits president to two terms.

**1952**—Dwight D. Eisenhower resigns as supreme commander in Europe and is elected president.

**1953**—Stalin dies; struggle for power in Russia follows. Rosenbergs are executed for espionage.

**1954**—U.S. and Japan sign mutual defense agreement.

**1955**—Blacks in Montgomery, Alabama, boycott segregated bus lines.

**1956**—Eisenhower is reelected president. Soviet troops march into Hungary.

**1957**—U.S. agrees to withdraw ground forces from Japan. Russia launches first satellite, *Sputnik*.

**1958**—European Common Market comes into being. Alaska becomes the forty-ninth state. Fidel Castro begins war against Batista government in Cuba.

**1959**—Hawaii becomes fiftieth state. Castro becomes premier of Cuba. De Gaulle is proclaimed president of the Fifth Republic of France.

**1960**—Historic debates between Senator John F. Kennedy and Vice-President Richard Nixon are televised. Kennedy is elected president. Brezhnev becomes president of USSR.

**1961**—Berlin Wall is constructed. Kennedy and Khrushchev confer in Vienna. In Bay of Pigs incident, Cubans trained by CIA attempt to overthrow Castro.

**1962**—U.S. military council is established in South Vietnam.

**1963**—Riots and beatings by police and whites mark civil rights demonstrations in Birmingham, Alabama; 30,000 troops are called out, Martin Luther King, Jr., is arrested. Freedom marchers descend on Washington, D.C., to demonstrate. President Kennedy is assassinated in Dallas, Texas; Vice-President Lyndon B. Johnson is sworn in as president.

**1964**—U.S. aircraft bomb North Vietnam. Johnson is elected president. Herbert Hoover dies in New York City.

**1965**—U.S. combat troops arrive in South Vietnam.

**1966**—Thousands protest U.S. policy in Vietnam. National Guard quells race riots in Chicago.

**1967**—Six-Day War between Israel and Arab nations.

**1968**—Martin Luther King, Jr., is assassinated in Memphis, Tennessee. Senator Robert Kennedy is assassinated in Los Angeles. Riots and police brutality take place at Democratic National Convention in Chicago. Richard Nixon is elected president. Czechoslovakia is invaded by Soviet troops.

**1969**—Dwight D. Eisenhower dies in Washington, D.C. Hundreds of thousands of people in several U.S. cities demonstrate against Vietnam War.

1970—Four Vietnam War protesters are killed by National Guardsmen at Kent State University in Ohio.

1971—Twenty-Sixth Amendment allows eighteen-year-olds to vote.

1972—Nixon visits Communist China; is reelected president in near-record landslide. Watergate affair begins when five men are arrested in the Watergate hotel complex in Washington, D.C. Nixon announces resignations of aides Haldeman, Ehrlichman, and Dean and Attorney General Kleindienst as a result of Watergate-related charges. Harry S. Truman dies in Kansas City, Missouri.

1973—Vice-President Spiro Agnew resigns; Gerald Ford is named vice-president. Vietnam peace treaty is formally approved after nineteen months of negotiations. Lyndon B. Johnson dies in San Antonio, Texas.

1974—As a result of Watergate cover-up, impeachment is considered; Nixon resigns and Ford becomes president. Ford pardons Nixon and grants limited amnesty to Vietnam War draft evaders and military deserters.

1975—U.S. civilians are evacuated from Saigon, South Vietnam, as Communist forces complete takeover of South Vietnam.

1976—U.S. celebrates its Bicentennial. James Earl Carter becomes president.

1977—Carter pardons most Vietnam draft evaders, numbering some 10,000.

1980—Ronald Reagan is elected president.

1981—President Reagan is shot in the chest in assassination attempt. Sandra Day O'Connor is appointed first woman justice of the Supreme Court.

1983—U.S. troops invade island of Grenada.

1984—Reagan is reelected president. Democratic candidate Walter Mondale's running mate, Geraldine Ferraro, is the first woman selected for vice-president by a major U.S. political party.

1985—Soviet Communist Party secretary Konstantin Chernenko dies; Mikhail Gorbachev succeeds him. U.S. and Soviet officials discuss arms control in Geneva. Reagan and Gorbachev hold summit conference in Geneva. Racial tensions accelerate in South Africa.

1986—Space shuttle *Challenger* explodes shortly after takeoff; crew of seven dies. U.S. bombs bases in Libya. Corazon Aquino defeats Ferdinand Marcos in Philippine presidential election.

1987—Iraqi missile rips the U.S. frigate *Stark* in the Persian Gulf, killing thirty-seven American sailors. Congress holds hearings to investigate sale of U.S. arms to Iran to finance Nicaraguan *contra* movement.

# Index

Page numbers in boldface type indicate illustrations.

## About the Author

    Jim Hargrove has worked as a writer and editor for more than ten years. After serving as an editorial director for three Chicago area publishers, he began a career as an independent writer, preparing a series of books for children. He has contributed to works by nearly twenty different publishers. His Childrens Press titles include biographies of Mark Twain and Richard Nixon. With his wife and daughter, he lives in a small Illinois town near the Wisconsin border.